HUE & NUMBER

WHERE ART STARTS WITH A NUMBER

Color-By-Number

1 THIS BOOK IS MORE THAN JUST A COLORING GUIDE - IT'S AN INVITATION TO RELAX, ENJOY CREATIVE CALM, AND EXPLORE YOUR ARTISTIC SIDE. EACH DESIGN IS THOUGHTFULLY CRAFTED TO BRING YOU JOY BOTH AS YOU PAINT AND AS YOU ADMIRE YOUR WORK. IT'S NOT ABOUT ACHIEVING PERFECTION; IT'S ABOUT FINDING JOY IN THE PROCESS ITSELF. LET YOURSELF BE INSPIRED, TRY SOMETHING NEW, AND SAVOR THE LITTLE DETAILS!

---

2 THE DESIGNS IN THIS BOOK ARE CRAFTED TO BE BOTH EASY TO FOLLOW AND ENJOYABLE TO COLOR. IF ANY FINE DETAILS FEEL A BIT SMALL, TRY USING A MAGNIFYING GLASS OR YOUR PHONE (MAGNIFIER APP) TO CATCH EVERY PART EFFORTLESSLY! KEEP IN MIND, THOUGH, THAT BECAUSE THE IMAGE IS SIMPLIFIED INTO SHAPES AND NUMBERS, THE FINAL RESULT WON'T MATCH THE ORIGINAL PRECISELY. BUT DON'T LET THAT HOLD YOU BACK - THIS IS ALL ABOUT ENJOYING THE PROCESS OF COLORING AND UNWINDING. YOUR ARTWORK WILL BE A MASTERPIECE IN ITS OWN RIGHT!

---

3 WE RECOMMEND USING COLORED PENCILS OR FINELINERS, AS THEY WORK BEST. HOWEVER, OTHER COLORING TOOLS ARE ALSO PERFECTLY FINE TO USE! CONSIDER USING A PAPER BEHIND THE PAGE TO AVOID BLEED-THROUGH. YOU CAN ALSO MIX YOUR OWN COLORS BY FOLLOWING THE CMYK VALUES PROVIDED (FOR A VALUE OF C=70, M=20, Y=10, K=5, THAT MEANS MIXING 7 PARTS CYAN, 2 PARTS MAGENTA, 1 PART YELLOW, AND HALF A PART BLACK). OF COURSE, YOU'RE WELCOME TO PICK ANY COLOR YOU ALREADY HAVE AND LOVE–THERE ARE NO HARD AND FAST RULES. LET YOUR CREATIVITY RUN WILD, TRY NEW THINGS, AND ENJOY THE CREATIVE PROCESS. THIS ARTWORK IS ALL YOURS!

HAPPY COLORING!

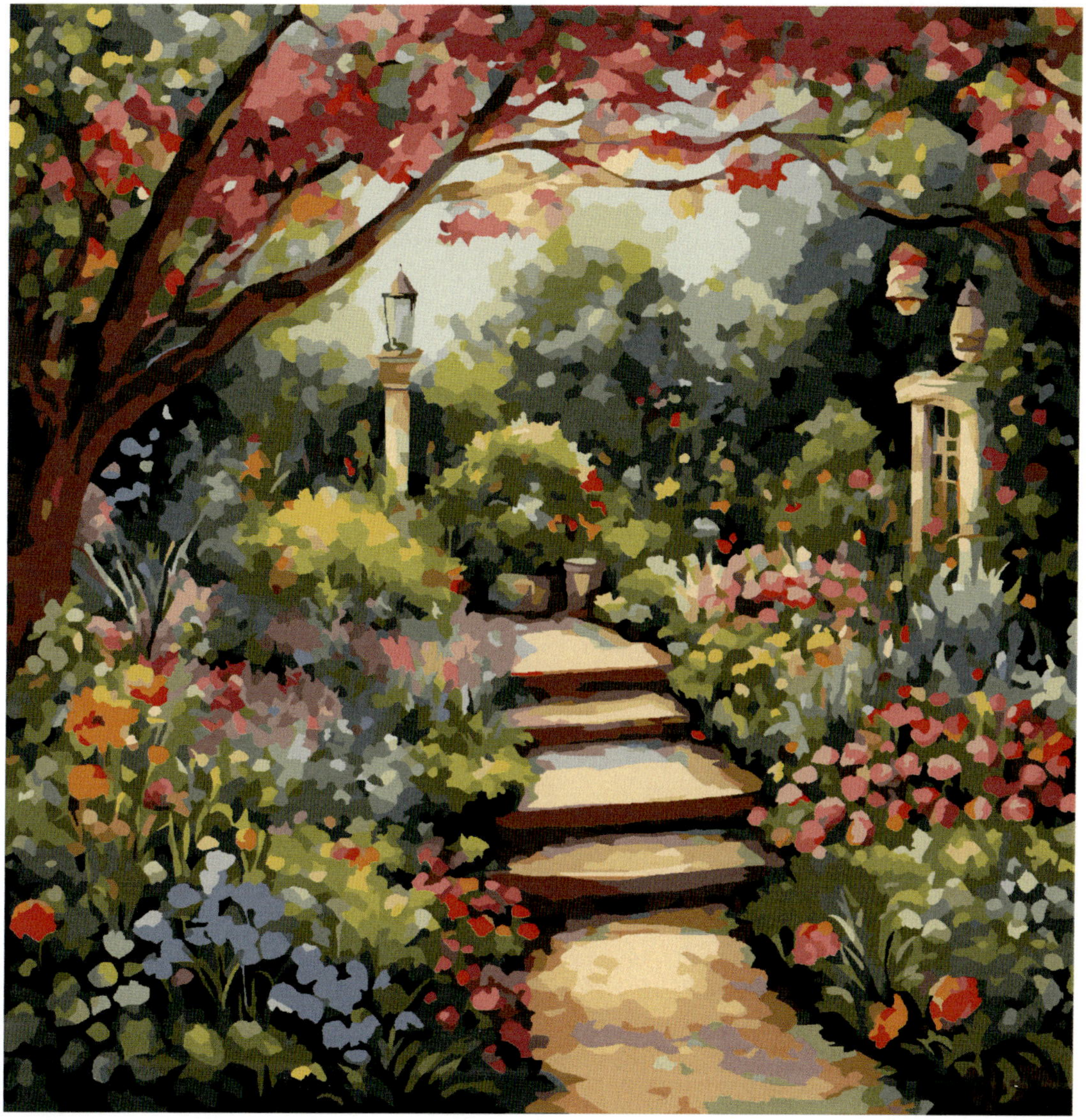

1	2	3	4	5	6	7	8
19,0,21,82	0,8,36,75	0,8,36,75	0,42,50,58	5,0,43,64	16,0,18,56	0,5,51,51	0,48,47,42
9	10	11	12	13	14	15	16
0,47,67,27	0,7,36,41	0,45,43,27	0,12,67,28	2,0,8,43	0,24,42,22	4,0,12,22	0,14,37,7

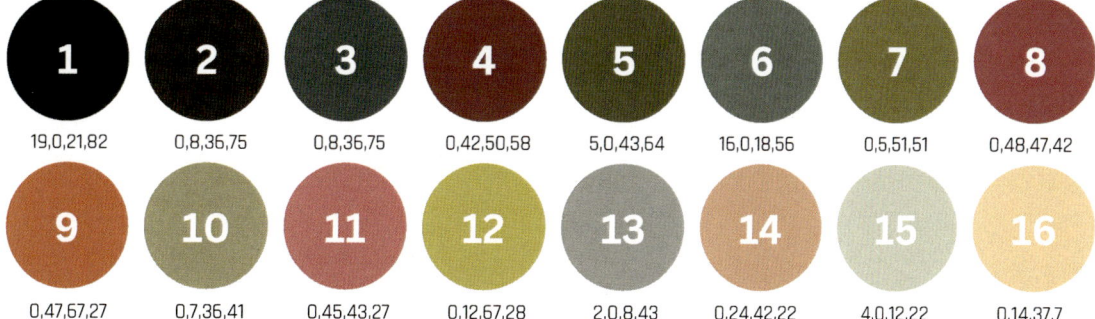

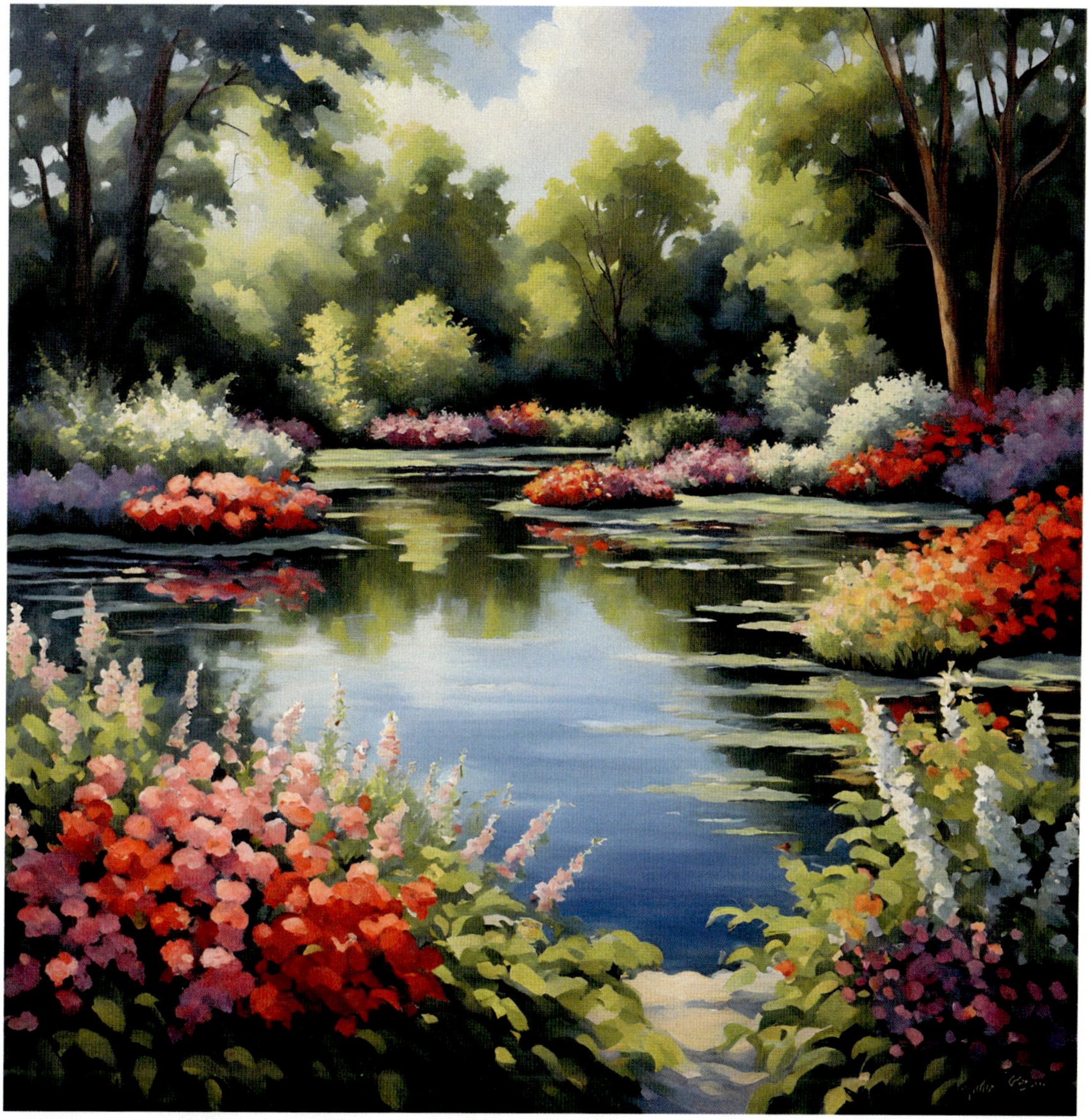

1	2	3	4	5	6	7	8
13,0,11,82	97,0,50,11	15,0,12,71	0,72,78,33	6,0,48,56	0,50,38,97	18,0,5,57	66,26,0,40
9	10	11	12	13	14	15	16
0,57,65,20	94,0,84,46	0,8,62,34	8,0,14,35	0,41,42,15	35,13,0,22	0,9,28,22	2,0,1,21

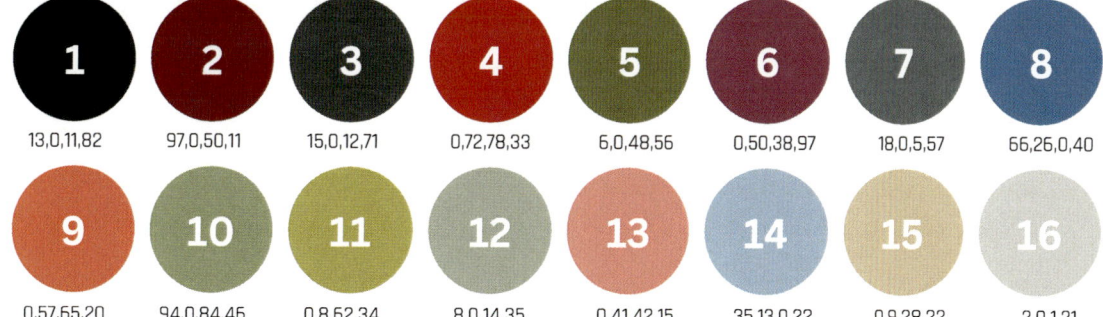

1	2	3	4	5	6	7	8
17,0,13,79	5,0,23,69	11,0,22,60	0,24,45,52	90,96,0,55	17,4,0,56	0,5,41,46	0,32,40,36

9	10	11	12	13	14	15	16
10,0,13,45	0,36,80,14	0,16,47,30	0,25,31,26	0,14,43,20	2,0,12,31	0,14,34,11	5,0,3,18

1 9,0,26,78	**2** 8,0,29,69	**3** 0,33,56,58	**4** 1,0,34,61
5 5,0,19,55	**6** 0,46,75,28	**7** 96,0,54,28	**8** 0,11,60,31
9 5,0,3,44	**10** 0,10,35,31	**11** 0,23,61,17	**12** 0,14,33,22
13 0,1,9,30	**14** 0,17,5,27	**15** 16,5,0,21	**16** 94,0,37,13

1	2	3	4	5	6	7	8
26,0,16,78	0,5,24,70	39,14,0,62	0,8,26,61	0,52,82,29	0,11,38,51	21,11,0,52	0,38,29,39

9	10	11	12	13	14	15	16
0,11,38,42	94,13,0,18	95,95,0,34	0,13,49,27	0,16,23,31	0,10,23,22	12,3,0,24	0,6,14,15

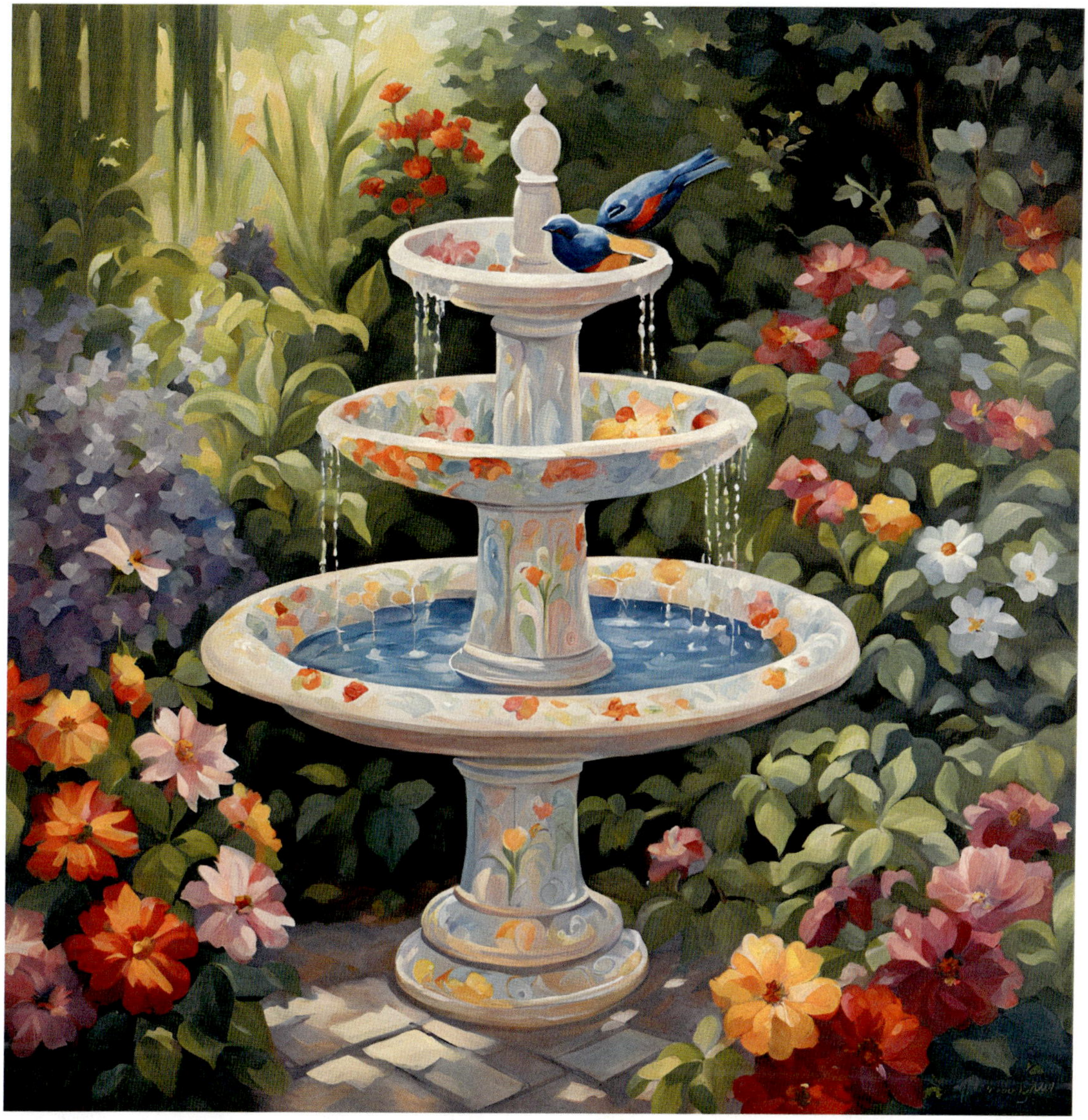

1	2	3	4	5	6	7	8
20,0,12,77	0,61,59,57	12,0,24,65	5,0,44,57	7,0,5,58	0,58,81,25	0,35,35,47	0,1,47,48

9	10	11	12	13	14	15	16
61,20,0,38	10,7,0,47	0,8,53,31	0,38,42,23	0,34,74,11	0,6,13,37	0,14,32,18	0,5,13,15

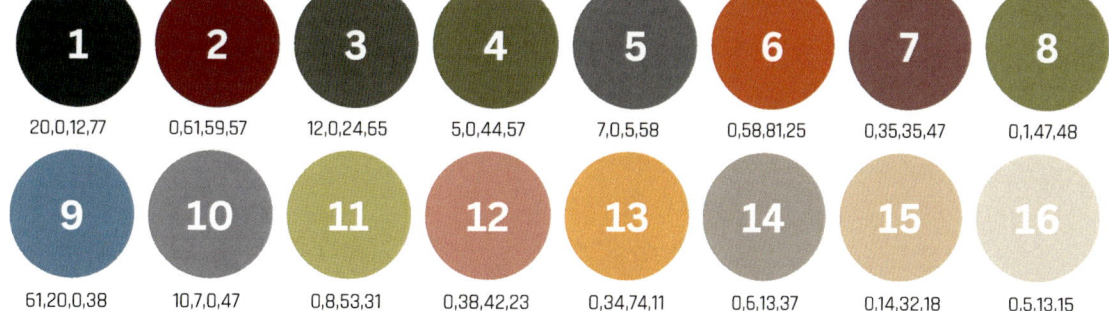

1	2	3	4	5	6	7	8
23,0,6,81	0,7,29,73	0,64,79,46	0,9,46,63	45,24,0,55	0,0,12,62	0,15,44,51	0,54,86,24

9	10	11	12	13	14	15	16
0,13,22,47	20,12,0,48	0,12,55,38	0,27,74,15	0,20,37,29	0,1,5,40	0,14,32,16	13,2,0,18

1	**2**	**3**	**4**	**5**	**6**	**7**	**8**
15,0,6,81	1,0,37,67	46,10,0,64	0,61,77,29	0,42,16,51	12,0,30,52	59,23,0,38	0,11,65,38

9	**10**	**11**	**12**	**13**	**14**	**15**	**16**
0,52,81,13	20,0,12,42	0,35,25,35	92,0,82,52	0,21,58,17	6,0,6,34	0,31,28,20	0,6,23,19

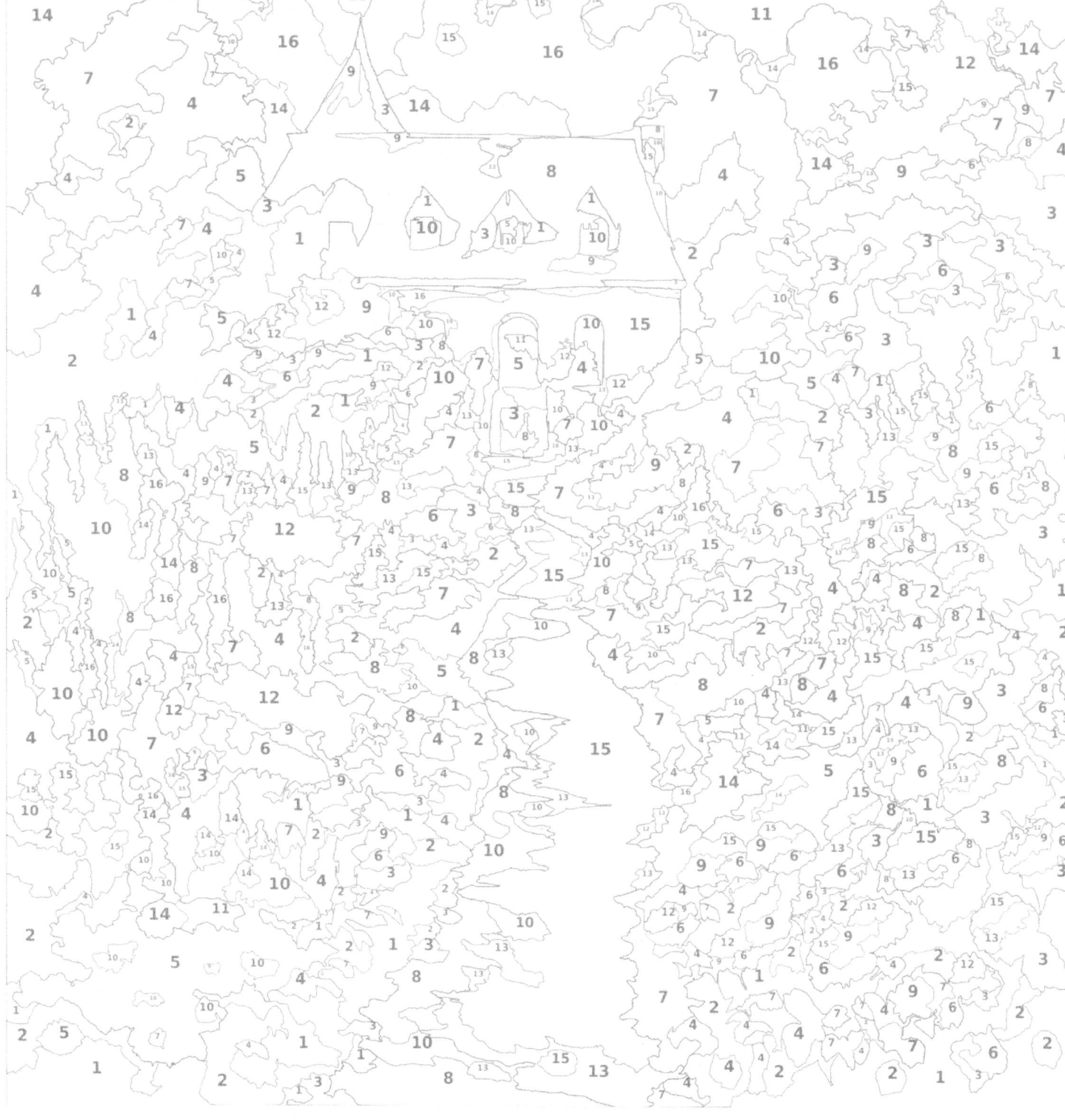

1	**2**	**3**	**4**	**5**	**6**	**7**	**8**
0,7,25,83	9,0,19,75	0,52,66,50	0,0,23,62	57,21,0,52	0,68,82,29	0,11,57,42	0,23,32,44
9	**10**	**11**	**12**	**13**	**14**	**15**	**16**
0,49,74,22	15,8,0,47	68,22,0,24	0,34,81,11	94,87,0,29	24,8,0,29	0,17,29,18	4,0,0,22

1	**2**	**3**	**4**	**5**	**6**	**7**	**8**
19,0,26,79	18,0,43,68	16,0,47,59	38,0,18,60	94,32,0,43	0,16,5,52	9,0,66,52	5,0,40,51
9	**10**	**11**	**12**	**13**	**14**	**15**	**16**
0,3,70,40	0,19,24,45	34,2,0,43	0,22,80,22	95,0,11,34	0,46,40,22	0,13,32,23	4,0,5,17

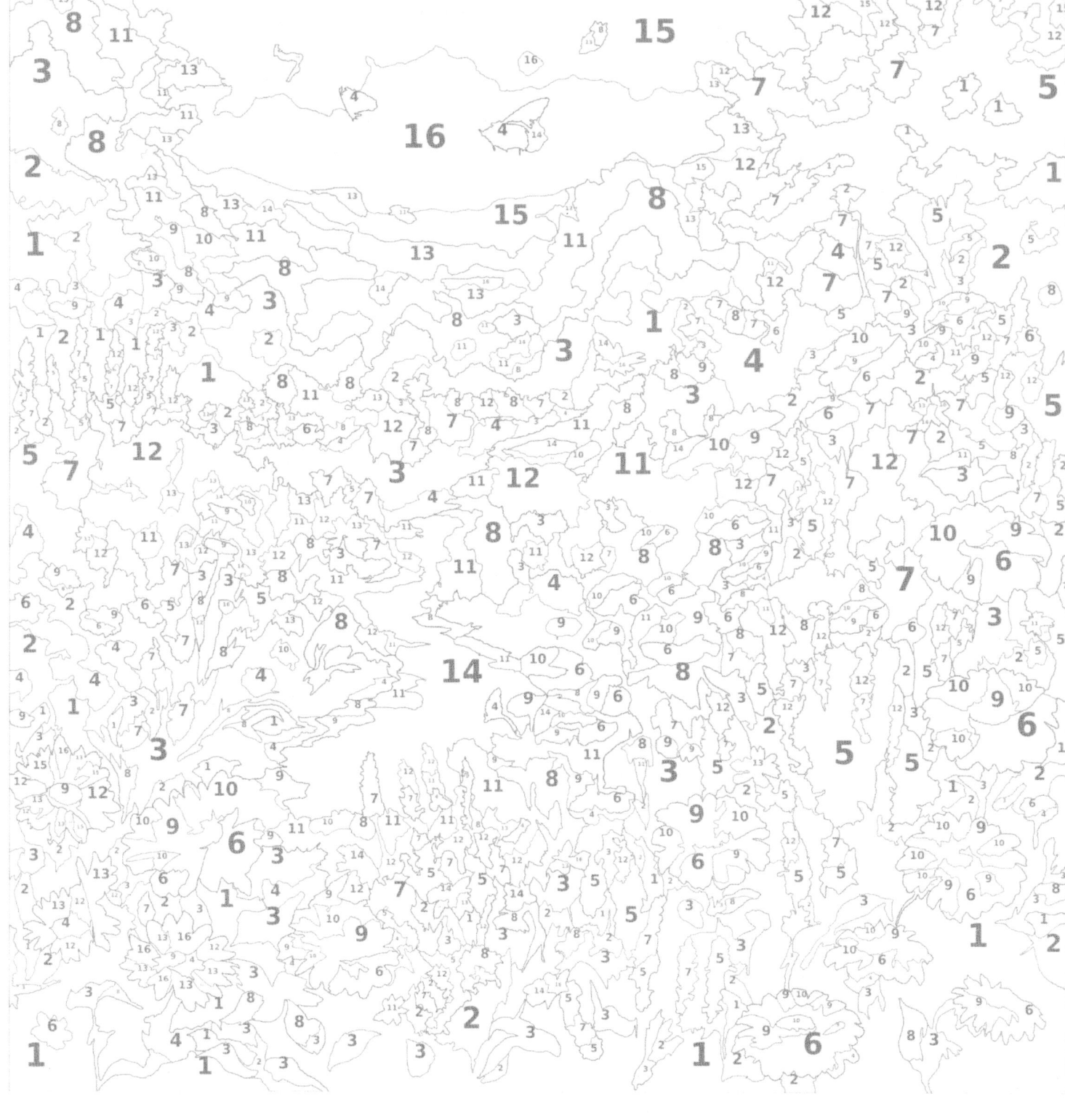

1	**2**	**3**	**4**	**5**	**6**	**7**	**8**
0,0,0,80	0,10,13,69	0,10,30,55	0,36,62,42	3,18,0,56	0,55,85,23	0,15,3,48	0,11,34,42
9	**10**	**11**	**12**	**13**	**14**	**15**	**16**
0,39,81,15	0,36,84,5	0,15,39,30	0,10,5,39	0,5,14,28	0,20,44,13	9,2,0,21	0,7,18,13

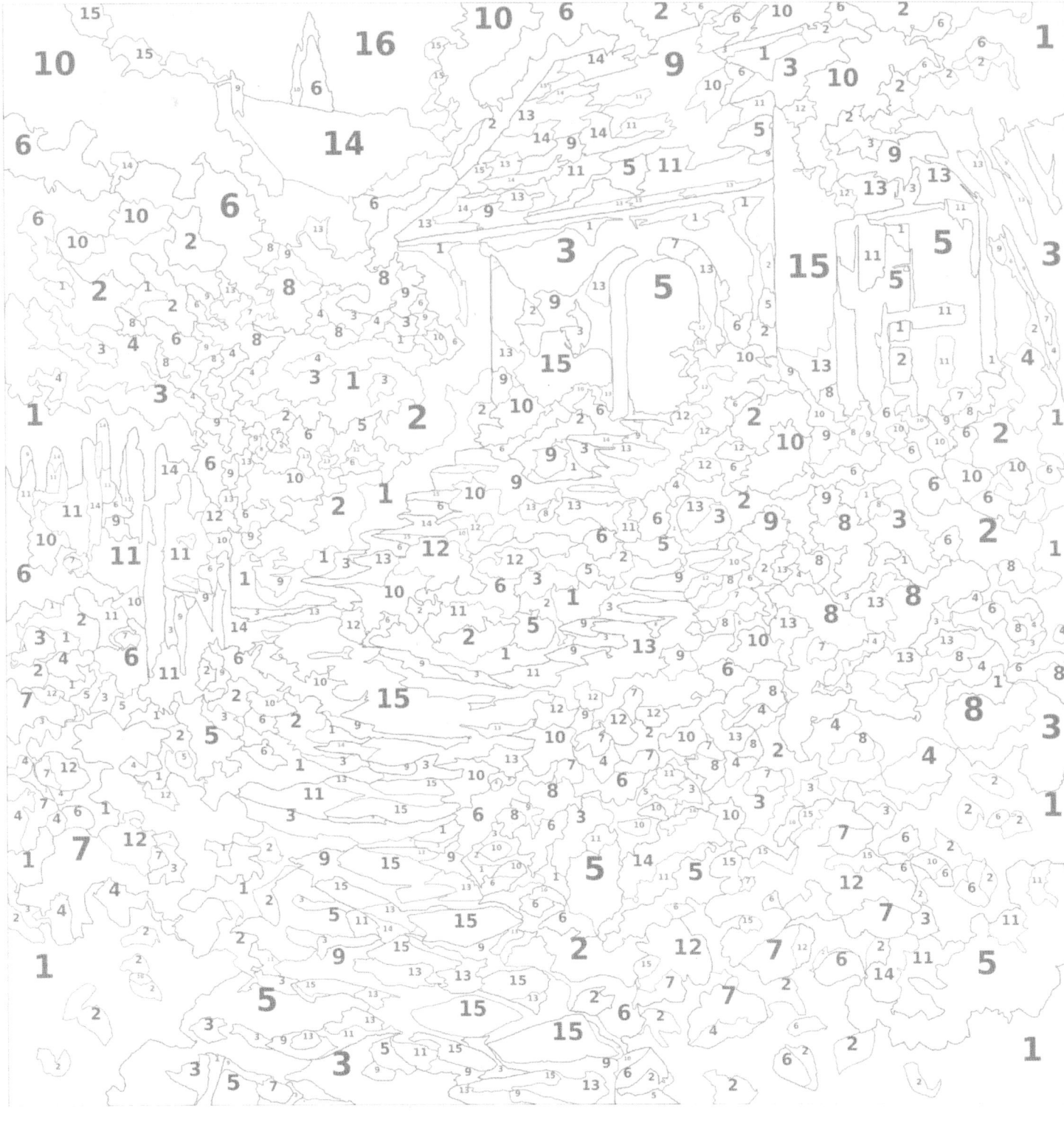

1	2	3	4	5	6	7	8
0,7,27,78	0,1,31,67	0,40,54,56	0,64,74,37	27,16,0,59	0,5,41,56	0,55,87,20	0,57,53,24

9	10	11	12	13	14	15	16
0,26,40,41	95,0,20,28	9,5,0,49	95,0,73,2	0,26,44,24	0,7,12,35	0,17,42,11	95,0,34,7

DID YOU ENJOY THIS COLORING
BOOK? WE'D BE THRILLED IF YOU
COULD TAKE A MOMENT TO LEAVE
US A REVIEW ON AMAZON–IT ONLY
TAKES 5 MINUTES! WHILE YOU'RE
THERE, FEEL FREE TO EXPLORE
MORE BOOKS IN OUR SERIES.
HAPPY COLORING AND
DISCOVERING!

HUE & NUMBER
WHERE ART STARTS WITH A NUMBER

Made in United States
Orlando, FL
14 July 2025

62953752R00019